AF580778

ABIDER

PITT POETRY SERIES

Nancy Krygowski and Jeffrey McDaniel, Editors

ABIDER

MELISSA CROWE

UNIVERSITY OF PITTSBURGH PRESS

Published by the University of Pittsburgh Press, Pittsburgh, Pa., 15260
Copyright © 2026, Melissa Crowe
All rights reserved
Manufactured in the United States of America
Printed on acid-free paper
10 9 8 7 6 5 4 3 2 1

ISBN 13: 978-0-8229-6837-5
ISBN 10: 0-8229-6837-1

Cover art: *Sister* by Sarah Jarrett
Cover design: Melissa Dias-Mandoly

CONTENTS

II.

III.

IV.

I swear, against my will I leave you.

—SAPPHO

ABIDER

I’ve Never Stopped Loving Anyone

I dream the moon breaks up, spray
of white splinters makes a haze across
the sky, wake expecting wreckage
to be real. Things fall apart, I know—
wounds so vast they never heal—
but everyone on whom I’ve rested
an eye rises nightly, whole and shining,
in my sight, mine a body suffused
with light from bodies that should
by rights have blinked out long ago.
It’s not that I grieve slow—my resting
heart’s a hummingbird, my love
a kind of endless blur. His sugar, hers,
brings me back and back to the yard,
so frequently it’s like I stayed. I sleep
hard in all the beds I’ve ever made.

1.

Why I Am a Poet

after William Stafford

Graves was the name of the mortician
in my hometown, the oil company
called Dead River—is it any wonder
I thought I could wring sense from
language, collapse the distance between
word and thing, the way a baby says
milk then tastes it? I learned to swim
in a lake named Echo, eight years old
in my baggy swimsuit with the keyhole
cutout, same suit I wore posed on a stage
that year, hoping for a beauty pageant
crown, somebody to say I was the best
girl—oh, bearable lightness of my body
finally afloat. Minnows nosed my ankles
then darted like a hundred little minds
changing. When I emerged, leeches
rode my thighs to land. And my life
again later, sixteen, parked at the lake,
I kissed the mouth of a boy headed
out of here until my lips burned—
you hear it, don't you? Echo? Echo?

I Never Touch the Stuff but Oh It Touches Me

He was a liar, my favorite uncle—claimed
a mother bear let him sleep with the cubs in her
cave, bragged he'd outrun the cops in every
state—and it felt good to believe him, get a little
of his sweet dream, felt wild my seventh summer
to let him lead me to the highway when he'd
been drinking all day, sundowning now into
scheme. He'd have wanted a hit of something
we didn't have on hand, said his new sweetheart
lived one town over, every pair of far-flung
Main Streets in that Big Wood linked by a stretch of
pavement like a silver bracelet hung with charms
the shape of potato-blossomed fields, tin-can
trailers in shades of sun-faded turquoise
and pink, each a paste gem set inside a circle of
junked cars. But we could see none of this from
the weedy shoulder on the night Larry taught me
how to hitch—it was dark. We'd only ride, he said,
with folks we knew. He sang Willie Nelson
in his slow, soaked drawl or told me scary stories,
bloody knives and monkey masks, while trucks
gusted and mosquitos swarmed and goldenrod
reached up my dress, until we found ourselves
closed in the cab of a stranger's pickup, ashtray
spilling and smoke filling my lungs and my uncle
complaining a little about my bony ass on his lap.
I wasn't exactly afraid. Certainly the driver had
a beer between his legs, one hand on the wheel
and a Camel in it, so to take a puff he had to
steer with his knee. Here's where memory almost

fails, so maybe we drive forever, and Larry's alive,
doesn't ever get high and wobble from his boat
and die, and I stay tiny, scratching my bug bites
and listening to men talk over the radio, dashboard
lit brighter than the moon through the windshield.
In at least one version, even I don't survive,
but let's say we arrive. I'm carried inside, sleep
hot under a jacket on the couch, wake to watery
light in a room I don't recognize. I'm alone in that
house or everyone's just passed out. I don't cry,
don't try to call my mother. If there's milk, cereal,
I eat while I wait for someone to come or come to.
I imagine my uncle returning, still smelling of booze
but sober enough to take me fishing, supply
the worms for my hook, burn bloodsuckers off
my ankles with a hot match. Already I want a story
to believe. Already the tender hour after dawn,
when the day may bring some sweetness we've
not tasted, is a spell I know better than to break.

I'm Tired of Writing About My Childhood

But I was born underground—or
I ate the seeds, and I can never leave,

not really. Which is to say I've seen your
moon, your sun even, how they hang

like lit fruit from a soft canopy of sky.
The wind that rounds the surface of this rock

ruffles my hair the way breath always does,
only yours is blossom scented, star jasmine,

sweet perfume. You smelled the dirt on me,
didn't you? Back at home, everything's

inverted—firmament of packed earth
and the only blooms are roots. You wonder

if we've gotten good at seeing in the dark,
consolation of adaptation? We're not like

lantern fish or frogs—ordinary bodies
ours, ordinary needs—but sometimes

we make out the shape of what's coming,
hold very still until the footsteps turn,

stop the rain of soil upon our heads.
Maybe I'm the poet of this place because

I like the word *gloaming* as much as *glimmer,*
how it holds both *glow* and *loam*, makes

of time a pageant, makes loss of light
another kind of light. I would write a sonnet

for daybreak, first beam by which you
watch your lovers leave—I like reprieve

as much as the next fool, am tempted by
the hand that reaches down, how sure

its fingers, its grip to me how dear—but
we're given our stories, same as our names.

I come how I'm called. I come from here.

I Want to Go to Them and Say Stop

after Sharon Olds

Thank god for the things I'll never
understand—what made my mother take

my father's hand across the decades
that separated them, across the carcass

of his marriage and the bar behind which
she worked, the one he sidled up to night

after night until whatever kept their bodies
apart—polite distance, obligation, fear—

dissolved. Then I began. He disappeared,
reappeared in his actual life, in the bed,

across the table from his wife. In theory,
a thing he'd planted grew. In theory, a child

like the ones he bathed and dressed and rocked
and soothed shot up under her mother's gaze

alone, and god, I've had my own child now,
I'll never understand how a man loves

only what happenstance keeps in his
eyeline, in his arms. Thank you, god, for

making me too stupid to make sense of
such a thing. When we met he said I looked

like her—that much makes sense—me the age
she was when he fucked her: eighteen. Watch me

watch him pull the plungers on a pinball game
in the bowling alley's back alley, move in

close enough to smell his aftershave. Catch him
caught off guard, watch his hands go still

but his eyes stay trained on the playfield,
bumpers and slingshots, bells and buzzers

stilled, and in that quiet my small voice:
I think you know my mother. I said it,

but I didn't believe it. Even now I can't
put them in the same room, never mind

a bed, a backseat, never mind this stranger
knowing anything about the body that grew me,

knew me first. *Who's your mother?* God,
the question made me want to fight, or fall down,

there's a universe in which I fell down, melted
through the floor, lived a whole stunned life

in the crawlspace underneath that room,
and here's my knees weak in this world, too.

I said her name. It's what I knew. Oh, god,
oh, Sharon, I want to live but can't press

that man against my mother for the spark
that starts me. She's instant rice with butter

or a bowl of cereal at night. She's cold hair
rubbed between my fingers to fall asleep

and the boot prints into which I put
my own small feet until we reached

some snow hill's peak and the speed
with which our bodies slid on plastic bags

and the silence in which we sometimes
sat a long time at the bottom, watching

the clouds our breathing made.
She's a hand towel warmed on the toaster

over and over and held to the throb
of my ear. She's waiting for me

at the bus stop. She fucks up. She's here.

The Men

The original man was an absence only. But it wasn't
him—not *gone*—I knew first. I knew the grandfather:
sandpaper cheeks, big-knuckled hands, silken forearms
lined in violet blue. He held me in his lap, held still
while I pressed those tender veins, stopped their
blood, then lifted my fingers to feel the pulse return.
Evenings I breathed his musk, sweat and hair oil,
kerosene, the sharp but fading perfume of his work.
This is how, when I was little, when I was lucky,
I received the body of the man or was received there,
without violence. Those nights, he was a woman with
an open hand. She waited for the bird of me to light.

I'm Not Mad at My Mother for Teaching Me How to Shave My Legs

She sat sidesaddle on the tub's edge, observing
the angle and pressure of my hold—my body,
after all, a small version of her own—advising
long strokes from ankle up and caution around
the tender tendon at the back of each knee,
instilling in me the terror of a loose limb
so I'm wobbled even now imagining that tether
slit. I don't blame her for the calm she kept
as I nicked and nicked, tiny stoplights of blood
blinking on against me, pale, and the ghost-
green water, going pink. I didn't have to be
cajoled or even comforted. She'd made me wait
till I was ten, first threshold meant, perhaps,
to stoke desire for a thing I'd otherwise avoid.
I'd begged permission, and though I barely
had the wherewithal to brush my teeth or change
my underpants, I'd keep myself sheered smooth,
careful half-botched session in the bath each week,
dry touchups before school, even winter mornings
when pants or fleecy tights concealed my work,
nothing but the rub of wool against this strange
new skin. I'm not mad at my mother, no. As if
unmaking's not the way a woman's made.
And so many eager hands to hold the blade.

Home Training

My mother didn't teach me to refuse a ride
on the back of a motorcycle or warn me off
the candy from any open palm, didn't say

I shouldn't stretch myself, top to toes, along
the body of another girl, didn't teach me
not to pass through the house of the neighbor

with the shabby above-ground pool, not to pay
the toll to swim in his backyard, and that toll
took its toll, but also I swam. She was nineteen

when I was born. The lover who made
her pregnant—married, middle-aged—liked to
drink in the bar where she served shots of Jack

in sheer harem pants over satin knickers,
and that's all I know about that. He was gone,
and what did *gone* give me? Fatherless rooms,

handful of formative years without the hairy
belly and bass voice and clipped commands
of a man trying to make me good. We lived

on a dead-end street near the old airport, vast,
cracked macadam where weeds grew waist high
and in winter skidoos revved their whining

engines so loud we heard them while we ate
our fried potatoes or watched *Three's Company*
on TV. Eventually I'd take sweethearts there

and press them into snow or flatten the tall
grass, kissing their mouths under the throbbing
sun. Come August, past chain-link my uncles

showed me how to break through, men set up
the fair with its Ferris wheel and Flying Bobs
and carnies who'd flirt with eighth graders,

give us free tickets, endless rides. The air
through my open window smelled like spun
sugar and axle grease, and evenings it lured me

to the fence for my fill of heavy metal music,
the Gravitron pressing me against its slanted
walls, my arms turned alien, pinned to my chest.

In the absence of the hovering love some kids
endured, I got up to things—in the woods,
by the railroad tracks, in backseats—I wouldn't

like to unlive. I'm not so wild anymore.
Even untutored, I learned how a woman's
meant to temper her hungers, cross her legs

and shut her mouth. But I taught myself to feel
good. Can't unlearn. My grown hand knows
its way to treasure. Tongue finds honey just fine.

Acceptance Speech

Camera cuts to me, holding the trophy
of my suddenly full-grown body, not
weeping or seeping under stage lights,
no blood-stained crotch or botched
makeup job, no bony knees or nipple
lumps showing through my too thin
tee, just this new me, looking like
I've never been struck dumb. I'm no
genius, not a star, but the close-up
shows my pimpleless face shining, how far
I've come.
                    And here it comes: I wish
to thank *Flowers in the Attic,* which I read
at my Nana's house while I had
chicken pox so bad sores erupted
everywhere—in my mouth, my ears,
I mean everywhere—and nothing
but twins fucking on a mattress
in an attic where their mother had
locked them so she wouldn't lose
the fortune she could only inherit
for some reason if she didn't have kids
could distract me from the endless,
maddening itch and my sadness over
missing the trip my stepfather had
taken my mother on. Even my baby sister
went along, sick with her own pox
but too little to be left behind, while
I was thirteen and could lie ignored,
covered in calamine and dog hair

on the couch, waiting for so many
kinds of relief.
                        Thanks, Susan's Market
and the lady with the short, platinum hair—
maybe Susan—who worked the counter
there, where I bought my penny candy
all through middle school, traded
bottles for coins and coins for nine
sweets at a time because tax kicked in
at ten cents. She never rolled her eyes,
just chewed her gum and counted
my FireBalls and Caramel Creams,
my Tootsie Rolls and Lemonheads,
with saintly, sexy patience. Maybe-Susan
smelled like Charlie and cigarette smoke,
and the skin above her V-necks looked
sunburned all year.
                            My thanks go, too,
to Tommy Gault, prettiest boy in
seventh grade, whose wide grin I saw
disappear just once, right before
the other boys stuffed us into a closet,
which was lightless, of course, completely
black, and I couldn't see his face at all.
He stayed so quiet it seemed possible
he might've gotten sucked into another
dimension like that girl in *Poltergeist*,
which I'd seen at a slumber party, movie
chaser to the horror of looking at an issue
of *Playgirl* we'd found in the field of

milkweed behind the apartment complex,
cowboy centerfold with his legs spread
on a pile of haybales, his one soft part
a mystery we gave up trying to solve
and turned instead to haunted TVs
and JoBeth Williams pressed to the ceiling
in her underpants and swimming pools
full of skeletons and kid-sucking closets,
but back to you, Tommy, and my aching
gratitude for the way you did nothing—
nothing weird, nothing mean—through our
whole shared sentence, our seven minutes
in heaven, though at the time, I'll admit,
I worried it meant there was something
wrong with both of us.
                                        Yes, I hear it,
the music—I'm almost done, I swear.
Just let me mention the nights I woke
swollen with terror, certain I'd grown
monstrously large in my sleep, stumbled
the hall to the room my mother shared
newly not with me, and my stepfather
grumbled, but she lifted her side
of the blanket and I slid in, trying
to explain—I'm both inside and outside
my body, my skin threatening to split.
Oh, shit—I was too big, too big now,
I understood, for the haven of my mother's
marriage bed, but she shushed me,
hummed a little, smoothed the damp

hair from my forehead, while the house
rumbled and the curtainless windows
pulsed with light—

thank you, fear,
tenderness, I could not have become
this, or much, without you—and I was
lulled, returned a final time to fitful
sleep by my mother's voice, her touch.

So What if I Was Born Wanting Both

the cloistered peace of a nun's bed—
to stretch nights on its thin mattress,

over its spare metal frame, her cell
silent and otherwise empty, its bare

walls white as chalk—and to sleep
my whole life wrapped like the body

of a slim snake, all muscle and skin,
around the body of another snake?

When I was a poor kid, a second life
glittered, shone and vanished at intervals

too quick to clutch. What I wanted,
what I understood I couldn't touch.

But what was to hand? I put my hand
on it, in my narrow bed, afternoons

I begged off middle school or nights
I lay awake, waiting for the house

to go quiet, eyes on the fat moon
through the window, that distant

light, and my body lit up, creature
just born, it seemed, from beckoning.

I had such patience then, faith
of the supplicant or the nomad

in the woods—furred or naked—
wanting heat. I'd never seen the face

of God or yet made fire by rubbing
sticks or flanks until they spark,

but I'd heard tales of clasped
or moving hands dispelling dark.

The gathering ache between my legs
and the lips I'd conjured, kissing mine,

made me believe I'd have myself
and love. Is this why lovers fear

we'll leave? Not Helen ferried
to the far shore or Eve fed sweetness

by some other hand—but hers?
A woman self-possessed commands

a moveable feast, and I'm the kind
of beast who might live simply,

coming and coming, in my solitary
cave. It's a thing I crave and those

coiled bodies, too. Want still
shimmers, these years later: to warm

my hands on self and, other, you.

Always I Have Been Trying to Show Her

this beauty, my body, and always there are other
eyes from which to hide, like that summer night

I spent with a boy and his mother in the one-room
cabin on the lake, feast of corn and grilled potatoes,

some '80s movie on the tiny TV, and then—
our limbs swim-tired—sleeping stalls, side-by-side,

his mother's bed in one, mine in the other, and him
with a clear view from his pallet on the floor.

Moonlight shone on me from a small high window
and must have lit the water, too, but we couldn't

see that shimmer, only this: me lifting my nightgown
slowly, him rising to his elbows, one eye on his

mother's sleep, both on me and wide with awe,
like a sailor born on ship, spotting the only land

he's ever seen. He'd told me weeks before
that the worst torture he could imagine

was finding himself on one side of a glass wall
and on the other a naked woman, and wasn't that

his life then, at fifteen—desire and barriers
to desire—and by torture, didn't he mean

an ache, prolonged and hungry ache, and didn't
he like it as I did, isn't that why for a long moment

I sat so still in secondhand glow before letting
my dress fall, cover my own light? If I'm wrong,

I'm sorry—if in this way we were not the same—
but I remember my breasts, perfect, pale and blue-

veined and pink-tipped, and I remember
that gesture as a gift. Anyway, I wasn't so cruel,

even then—next morning when he asked me
to walk in the woods, float beside him in the old

canoe, I did, and there in sunlight tempered only
by the lace of leaf shadow, accident of passing

cloud, I let him see me again—touch me—and if
there were other eyes in the world, I let myself forget.

Who Is Responsible for the Suffering of Your Sister?

after Bhanu Kapil

Bhanu, what if it's me? I remember her rocked
through the gloaming, our mother singing *hush*
little baby, and if a child that small can feel sorrow,
my sister did, fat tears and a keening cry, as though
she'd come to us from another time, carrying
a splinter of memory on which the tender song
pressed. What comfort to imagine she'd arrived
with her grief, harmed elsewhere and not
by my own hand. How have I hurt my sister?
She counts the ways: refused to bathe with her
once my nipples turned acorn and crotch went
moss—the privacy I yearned for felt to her like
theft. Stopped sleeping in the bed we shared,
took to the floor to practice my own quiet keen,
so she was robbed again of the safety or at least
the warmth my body leant. Kept leaving, girls
it seemed not meant to cleave to each other for
long. She cried at my wedding, too—in fact, a whole
row of sisters cried in the sunlit clearing where
I said my vows. Suddenly, Bhanu, I had so little
patience for what softness tried to keep me still.
To go, I thought, was to grow, and so I did. I do.

I Trust You

And it's like the time I was reading on the lawn,
saw motion from the corner of my eye, and turned
to find—to think I'd found—my dog killing a small
brown bird that spasmed in the grass. I started
to cry. No, I said, no, no, no, no and Leave it.
I hadn't seen the dog touch the bird, just her
springing around its body the way she does with bugs,
small hops, tentative dips of her nose toward where it lay.
But for a moment, I believed her capable of a violence
I'd never glimpsed in her, believed a creature
I'd so long loved might, in my own front yard, commit
murder. I leaned over the bird, its breast heaving,
one black eye shining up at me, then a sudden thrust
toward flight, but it couldn't get much air. Mostly just
lay there, my good dog now sitting where I'd told her to,
on the porch steps, not mad for the bird's blood. Gentle.

Dear Life

> I was bred for slaughter like the other
> animals. To suffer exactly at the center,
> where there are no clues except pleasure.
>
> —Linda Gregg

It's raining hard, and we're moving slow over a blurred
road we don't know. My husband won't pull over,

keeps both his hands on the wheel, and my grip's
stubborn as always, on what I've chosen and on what

I think I shouldn't show. Lately my inner weather
takes the shape of imagined betrayal, mouths I'll swear

when the storm has passed I've never kissed.
But there's this urge to confess: that I've already

risked our lives, that sometimes when I call her *buddy,*
I mean *baby.* Anyway, we drive, or my betrothed does,

and I face the window and cry, let's say for the roadkill
that litters this stretch like a crumb trail I don't want

to follow, like the landscape reading my hidden palm.
It doesn't matter if the thing I think is a body is only

a half-empty garbage bag slumped near the centerline,
dirty blanket in the breakdown lane. As we near,

I expect to be relieved, but a mirage is the specter
of a thing that's real so I still feel the real thing's loss.

This pile of leaves and sticks not being fur and bone
doesn't make all the rabbits rise up, reconstitute,

reach the clover their hunger made them seek.
I remember a pastor telling me when I was maybe nine

that animals can't go to heaven, and at twelve I saw
some man on TV say the same about me, illegitimate,

unredeemed, my mother's own original sin.
I could turn, easy, and say all this to the man who

loves me, maybe find myself on a smoother
road, but like the other animals, I'm trapped here,

where the brutal end is everywhere visible. And, sure,
could be I'm crying because the bodies of raccoons

and possums matter as much as my own smear
of feathers on tar, enough to mourn if not forgive,

or maybe it's as simple as this: what if I'm so hungry
I make of my dear life a disaster? Just a little weather

and this whole road's wreckage—busted Stuckey's sign,
mangled fence around the horse farm, and the doe

we had no hand in making dead but which after
a hundred rain-soaked miles I can't stop

seeing. *Buddy*—I want to believe it's not all
bad news, I do. And just now I'm remembering

a morning I woke early, left my marriage bed
to sit in the backyard with my tea, soon startled

to find, to think I'd found, three dead blue jays,
their wings bent strange and spread against

the pine straw at the base of the loblolly I keep worrying
will fall on our house. I mourned them until there was

nothing in my mug, but it turned out they were taking
the sun, storing heat in their feathers for the day

ahead, and when they were done, they did the thing
we can't stop wishing we could do—they flew.

In the Other Universe, I Have a Bear Tattoo

she traces with her finger, or where her finger
moves the bear appears, baring now its belly,
now its teeth, fierce and eager creature only
she commands. And here? Do I wear the same
wild shape—invisible—in this world, too, where
I do not know her hands? And if I say I do—?

The Thing Itself

"A [ ] is not a hybrid of anything."

—Brian, San Diego, USA, "Notes and Queries,"
The Guardian

You know the fruit I mean.
Friend, I won't name it since you
asked me not to, but I can't

help dropping adjacent
honey here: words like *freestone*
or *clingstone*, self-fruitful

and with seeds that carry
the recessive allele
for smooth skin. Yes, peaches

for kin, same syrup, same
perfume, just a lucky
deviation sometimes

budding furless from the selfsame
tree, brilliant golden yellow
with a blush of red, its pink-

tinged meat a little firmer
to the touch than, say, the vaunted
plum, which I have eaten,

yes, delicious, but which, no matter
what Kate from Potters Bar
or Jane from Bethel has to say,

constitutes no portion
of this particular
body christened in the drink

of the gods, its name—like
yours—a metaphor
for refusing to disappear.

You know, don't you, that nature
holds you close and finds no
fault with you? And what about me,

my desires inventing new
desires? What about the apple,
which in Latin shares the word

for evil and which, though in such
abundance lies our choice, we evoke
so much it comes to stand

for any fruit that's juicy and bears
seed—sibling peach and common
fig—not to mention

illicit knowledge, not to mention
godless death. Anyway, I'm
glad some woman tasted it, let

the rest of us know
how sharp the fall,
how sweet the flesh.

Second Person

Girl in eighth grade with honey hair cut blunt
at your jaw and sprayed into wings that framed

your handsome face, you asked if I knew how
to *French kiss,* and the curve of your bottom lip

made me believe I did. Some set of sudden
muscles flexed, and because I said yes,

you arranged for me to meet at playground's
edge my boyfriend, eager in his scout uniform,

starched kerchief knotted at his neck,
and in my throat a knot rose, too—

I ached for his agent. I thought it was you
whose tongue I'd taste near the chain-link,

soles of our sneakers melting into hot top
and what else might melt I didn't know.

I do not know. But I can summon your wool-
and-woodsmoke curls, young man in my theater

troupe who handwrote poems about my face
under stage lights, *never more beautiful*, about the soft

at the back of my neck. I held you helplessly
one last summer while my fiancé slept in his

childhood bed a thousand miles away,
and before we parted you parked your father's

car in the field where in a few weeks there'd be
a Ferris wheel. Riding it, I'd recall the flip

in my belly when you said you feared we'd
never make love. We won't—but here you are

again. And college friend, I tucked you under
blankets on the couch of my first married

apartment, felt you tremble in that sweetened
dark. Yes, I stepped away, slid into bed

next to my beloved, but first I leaned over you
a cosmic hour, saying nothing, holding still.

And still I think about you, older woman
in the Memphis airport, layover and your legs

stretching toward me beneath the table
while we waited in the bar for the planes

that would take us each to our own elsewhere.
We exchanged addresses and I wrote to you,

once, twice, then gave up what I'd glimpsed,
your eyes hot on me like stars already dead

by the time I see their light. It's a cliché,
I know, this thing that shines so distant

we can't tell when it blinks out. But I get
scared of your absence sometimes, like it might

mean the end of a sky filled with beacons,
everything going dark while I look away.

Not in the sense that you aren't the sun,
only that I'm a planet far-flung in my orbit

or that I spin my days around another one.
Not in the sense that you could not have

been mine, my skin so warm it's glowing,
look, my skin on fire all the time.

What I Wanted to Keep Private

I wanted you last night when I woke, my body
vibrating like train-shook ground, and might have

let out the train's slow scream, the kind that quickens
as the beast draws near, but I wanted to keep private

that desire and that fear. Once, I transgressed
but I'm not a *permanent monster* is a thing a friend

said to comfort me for some sin of my own,
but in the dark that phrase travels me like a pulse,

shocking each cloistered organ in turn. When I was
fifteen, I took my grandmother's gold necklace

and gave it to a sweetheart, bit of shimmer
that graced my favorite neck until it slipped off,

sunk in the silt of a summer lake, lost, and I lost
the sweetheart, too, but I carried the lead-weight

shame of that theft, secret, until now. I don't feel
any lighter. I don't know what I might yet steal,

though I remember everything stolen from me,
like the kitten loosed from our house in the morning

and by afternoon purring in the arms of a neighbor kid
who swaggered up the driveway, invited me

to stroke his new cat. It's not so hard to forgive
that boy. Who doesn't sometimes want to hold

a soft thing not his own? Who doesn't hope
to know the sugar name that calls the handsome

stranger home? Anyway, I'm not alone. Once,
I was the kind of monster who takes the gold

from one beloved throat to trim another. Once,
I was the kind who hid the hunger that drives

my hand, as though only a said thing's made
true. Now? I love you. I just want to be said.

En Plein Air

How we came away burning.
How we stretched in the sand.
How the beak of the tern
dipped the sea like a hand.

How she hovered above me
to shield me from glare.
How I thought I might melt
from the fact of her there.

How the sunlight flashed golder
in the rounds of her eyes
and the water came lapping
the meat of our thighs

so we kept inching duneward
to resettle ourselves
on the blanket she'd brought
with our limbs and our shells.

How the afternoon's longing
came slow and then sharp
and the wind played my spine
like the box of a harp.

How the hours moved hungry.
We did not get our fill.
How we came away burning.
I'm burning still.

Interpenetration and Extension

I believe in science, which dictates two bodies
can't occupy—even briefly—the same space.
What did Descartes say? Annihilation.
But in the bathtub, which seems a quiet pocket
outside time and laws, I tell myself two truths
and a lie, out loud: I love him. Also her.
And if I love both well enough, it will be fine.
I believe in science fiction—membrane thins
and lovers leave a broken world for one
where they can touch without fear. Why can't that
be here, I whisper, but I already know. Even
in the movie, demons follow our sweethearts
through the breach, from home to hideaway,
from honeymoon to catastrophic wound.
No matter. It's clear I can't escape since
I am, myself, the overcrowded place. Ancient
Archytas wondered hard—if somehow
he arrived at heaven's furthest edge,
could he not extend his hand into whatever's
outside what we've taken to be true?
I remember reading that atoms repel each
other such that no two objects ever really meet.
How close, then, can I have been to him?
How close might my hand yet come
to hers—how close—before I break the skin
around what's so far passed as real? Since
physics tells us we can never touch,
perhaps there is no reason not to try? To feel?

When It's Over

Strangers touched me inside, this time with a large bore
needle. They told me when it was over. I didn't get

to say. Not when it hurt a little, not when it hurt a lot.
When they pushed the fentanyl, I thought, *Oh, I'm afraid,*

the way I might notice, then name, a butterfly lighting
on a blade. My first narcotic and suddenly, little brother,

I understood what you wanted. I forgave. Later woke
lighter, knowing there'd never been a sin against me,

though, yes, I'd suffered, and you were sorry for so long.
What a way to live—me in your story, you in mine.

The summer you turned five, you started hiding,
in the old blanket chest, underneath the bed.

You thought the shots you got for kindergarten
would happen every day, jab or two with morning milk,

and you couldn't imagine anything sweet enough
to make you take and take such pain. We explained

you were all caught up, no more shots for years,
but it didn't calm your fears. You got sick on the bus,

lingered so long in the boys' bathroom the janitor
had to fetch you out. One day you walked the blocks

back home, unwitnessed flight, teacher's gaze distracted
by a fight. I wasn't there, just married, so I don't know

how long you waited, freezing on the porch, before
a neighbor called our dad at work, but here's a fact:

your pinkie toes went black. Now a hole between my ribs
through which maybe self-righteousness slid, along with

the pieces of meat they snipped from me, whole drugged
minutes during which I slipped—finally—from the grip

of myself, though nothing blurred but me. The room
stayed sharp, and scalpel, too. *Can you feel it?* he said,

and I meant to ask *Feel what?* but I said no. Brother,
I felt everything and still held still for carving.

Seems like you know how to quit a thing that hurts
but only by exchanging it for something worse. Mine's

a different curse. I can't quit anything. Even now.
When the tests came back, they said no more booze,

for life—three pills a day, clean living, and for a while
I'll keep the liver I was born with, the one my body

wants to kill, the one that seems to mean me ill—
and I had to laugh. Hadn't I abstained since birth?

Tonight's a first. I'd once have walked wide-eyed—
yes, sober—into flames for more of what I've got

right now. I counted the ways on the way to the table,
replayed one kiss and thought *remember this*, as though

I'd take a memory to grave or maybe here, where fear
might make me make a bitter trade, too-bright worry

for some darker shade, might make me think,
oh brother, how well played your hand and every

hand before us, forefathers and uncles whose livers
conked out, too, who maybe forewent sober life

not to swallow something so sweet they'd risk
death for one more taste but because life hurts

too fucking much to do it dry. Do I get to say
when it's over? Brother, I'm scared. I'll try.

This One's Going to Be About Birds

All spring house finches try to nest on our
front porch. Through the window, I see and see
the scene unfold when I sit on the sofa with
my spouse. Above a pillar, there's a sheltered
place, flat, maybe eight by eight. We hardly use
that door. It's quiet. Seems safe, I'm sure, to little
birds, pair after pair, plain but for the flush
of pink at their necks. The female lays some twigs,
then sits and gives a gentle shake—this is a test—
and all she's woven, every time, comes loose.
She tries again, same result, too little room,
margin insurmountable but slim, so they can't
ever tell at the outset, only after all morning's
toil. Soon as I spot her, as though I've arrived
from the future, I say *It won't work*, but we don't
speak the same language. She keeps on until
her smallest move makes all the pieces fall.

Upon Learning They Dress Up as Bears to Take Care of the Motherless Cub at the Zoo

I start to cry. The kit's not convincing,
brown sweats and a plastic mask that would

scare the shit out of you if you opened
the door to it on Halloween night,

the kind you might see in footage from
a robbery, whole gang of fake bears waving

guns and demanding all the cash in the till—
they want everything you've got. I wonder,

do these fake bears coo? Does a baby bear
like the same noise our own kids get, all that

encouragement for not much, rolling over
or eating a spoonful of cereal, looking

adorable and mostly helpless all day long?
Does he get a song, this orphaned animal—

hush, little baby or the wheels on the bus?
He must. These jokers are willing to arrive

in costume to soothe him. Surely, they sing.
Or maybe they have to growl? I could google

mother bear sounds, but what fucks me up
most is that it doesn't matter—he's so

easily convinced. Jesus Christ. Me, too.
What's the difference between tenderness

and trickery, so long as somebody's
willing to pretend to be what you need?

He wants to be loved, so he takes any sign.
Puts himself at the mercy of what paws arrive.

Cold Turkey

They say to stop drinking, take the medicine.
I stop. I take the medicine, but I stop taking

your directions, too. Soon you say we're
incompatible, that before you can leave

we must move through the items on a list—
groceries, bills, telling your mother, telling

our child—and I put apples into the cart,
stare at the spreadsheet, sit next to you

on the sofa while you instruct the human
we made: *If you want me, call. Don't*

text me. I hate texting. I take the medicine.
When you say goodbye, I say it too

and watch you move through the door,
body I've known since I was myself

a child. Through the window I watch you
back out of the driveway, disappear,

as I have so many times, expecting your quick
return. What now? There's the doctor's

voice still in my head. There's yours,
of course, clear as the writing on the bottle.

But for hours on the first day, I don't hear it.
Some other sound seems about to emerge,

as if from a dark lake. I swallow nothing.

In the Wilderness

For forty nights after he leaves, I watch
a woman brush another woman's hair
on YouTube, drift off to one slow

finger tracing a spine in candlelight,
grazing the line where bare skin borders
silk. But when their sibilant whispers

cut out, I startle, fine-tuned now
to culmination. Alert to shifts from
sweetness to whatever happens

next. I mark the dawn of each of
forty days by coming and then crying,
the young locksmith next door no doubt

privy to my groaning and my sobs.
I don't realize how thin the wall
we share until he takes up drumming,

tuneless clamor rattling my room.
I don't blame my neighbor or myself.
We're practicing. My best friend says

recalibration, grief and pleasure wires
crossed in me. I'm grateful for this
grace. I'm not the god who saves

by suffering. This season's pain
is only pain—and mine. This hand
is not an angel's hand—but kind.

I Still Have to Try Not to Call You

Wasn't it so cold when you called past
midnight that first time, to read from
Flannery O'Connor and to say my name
like a password while I lay in my twin bed,
winter breaking in through broken glass?
Wasn't it so, so cold, and didn't you want
me open, skin of my breast pinned apart
to reveal a thing so common I won't even
name it here. And didn't I open, finally,
before my stepfather picked up downstairs
to order fuel we couldn't afford, beg the guy
at Dead River to come and bleed the tank?
And damned if I didn't hear Dad's voice—
Hello?—and hang up my end, leave you
crooning *Melissa* in his ear. But when the oil
arrived, blessed heat banging its way
back into our rooms, didn't I call and beg
to hear you say my name again? In physics
I'd learned a piece of paper folded enough
times will theoretically reach the moon.
Didn't I, still shivering, believe your voice
could reach me? Didn't I know it would?

The Speaker's Husband

I kill cockroaches now. We used to team up—
I'd fetch the postcard and the glass so you could
make the clean catch, then I'd open the door,
you'd set the cowboy free. We called them

cowboys then, trying to love them a little.
Look—I'm telling you what you already know,
surest sign I'm not really talking to you. *Were I*
with thee, cried Emily—it's called apostrophe—

and Keats lamented bodies etched in urn could
never kiss, but in direct address he made the frozen
lovers burn. To the infant daughter who could not,
of course, talk back, Anne Sexton wrote, *I made you*

to find me. I can't stop writing like this, as if I want
some way of being witnessed without ever
seeing you again. I keep forgetting not to leave
food on the counter. I've read how roaches

remember and return to nutrition sources.
I make a source, like a promise, and when I lift
the bag of bluing bread or the gone-soft orange,
they scurry the counter, I bring down

the wooden spoon. I got a tattoo, forearm
full of beautiful blooms. You'd hate it,
but I want to explain the steady scrape,
like scratching a mosquito bite on a sunburn—

it hurts, but you don't want to stop. Sometimes
when I think about your body, it's like you've
died and sometimes the more painful thing is
knowing you're alive and sometimes I'm startled

into absolute peace. This version of me
doesn't wish to touch the you who you turned
out to be. I only miss the one who doesn't
exist. David Hume claims desire motivates action

but logic selects the course. If I spot on a high bow
an apple that looks delicious, I'll climb the tree,
but if I discover the fruit is rotten, I won't
put my mouth to it. I no longer desire your body,

but some days I long for the woman
who did, who climbed and climbed, believing
in the sweetness beneath the skin. I've spent
most of my life believing one of us would

be wrecked by the other's death. So romantic,
all that dread. Then I heard the phrase *buried
in the same hole* and was soothed—a thing to look
forward to—but there's the hole you won't

stop digging, asking me to lie inside, alive.
Maybe I've stopped fearing death because
I don't need to outlive you to be free.
It's a good theory, only you've just texted

to say you have Covid, and here you are, flesh-
and-blood man I understand is not the man
I imagined him to be. You're sweating in your
sleep. Coughing. Tugging the hand I didn't know

I still extend. I say it out loud to keep from
texting you back. I write it down: you do not
need me. It is not me you love. One night
when we'd been dating only weeks and me

sixteen, we argued in the street while a friend's
van idled, waiting to take me to a dance you didn't
want me to attend. You held my arms and said,
When I say I want to be with you, I don't mean

I want to be with you. I mean I want to be you.
When I'm too tired to cook, I order dinner
and wait with the front door open, breathing
on the storm door's glass. I'm sad, but I'm hungry.

I'm scared, but I'm lonely, so I've summoned
a stranger with food. When he arrives, I almost
tell him these are my pajamas from last night
because I loved a man for thirty years, and then

we disappeared. These days you drive for Lyft.
You tell your rides about me, our marriage,
my career. Did you know *doppelganger* once named
a kind of ghost, *double walker*, near twin who haunts

the living flesh? Frogs like to sleep between
the doors of my rental, and last night while
I waited for my pizza, one jumped onto me,
leapt away as quick but not before I felt

the softness of his whole, impossibly light
body on the skin of my forehead, like if rubber
were silk but less substantial, little slip of
embodied tenderness, only time that I've been

touched in weeks. When we parted, you asked
if I'm *going to be gay now*, and I said I'm what
I've always been. Now I wonder, while you
talk to the women you pick up at the airport,

their bags in your trunk, their soft hands
tucking twenties into yours, are you making
her, the speaker's wife, to find you? She can't
find you. Sometimes I miss him so much. Jesus,

it's awful what we both know now. Even our dead
ringers, immaterial, misaligned, can never touch.

Multiverse Elegy Ending with the Dream in Which She's Mine

We met in the wheatfield, remember?—
  or the rye or in the mineshaft or the shaft
of light some moon shot down through
  thickened air that might be water, we met

underwater, holding breath or teacups—
  both—cross-legged at the bottom
of the city pool, sipping with our pinkies
  up, lit green and leaden till we couldn't last

without a suck of air, we met at the fair,
  throwing darts for bags of goldfish,
spun stupid with our mouths full of hair,
  our hips pressed through the fireworks,

waterworks, you cried and I kissed you
  goodbye before I knew your secret
name, we met hunting game, wild antelope
  and elk, big meat beasts, and us hungry

arrows, well nocked, we met to the thud
  of our heads in hides or rifle blasts and then
the blade, its whispered renting, skin
  from skin, we met by the fire, burnt fat

on the tongue, in the tent, and us so young,
  so eager, so undone, we met on a distant
planet's dying sun—or near it, another
  anthropocene, in a future so bright

we kept our eyes shut tight till the conductor
  called it safe, and anyway we did or didn't
vaporize inside the capsule where our
    lucky tickets put us close but either way

the heat that leapt between us found me
  crazed, my fingers grazed your fingers'
tips, we met like muzzles, over the fence
  that split our fathers' farms, or you

tattooed my arms, I strolled into the parlor
  where you'd plied your craft your whole
damn life and me on shore leave or fresh
  start, my sleeve in need of one more bottled

ship or broken heart, we met, we met. We
    meet tonight in my sleepy town, under
the only streetlamp's cobalt glow. I'm telling
    this story. Trust me, love. You do not go.

It's Not the Body's Fault

but mine is where the ache resides, site of a thousand delicate
harms—soft of a cheek on the soft of a cheek—and hers
a door upon which I try and try not to knock. Yes,
remembering hurts, though I won't indict the jaw, skin
of the wrist, belly or its button, little hollow where the tongue
in my mind still dips, conjuring the ghost of a moan from
the mouth I have ceased to kiss for good. I don't blame
the hands, not mine or hers, not the animal they made
when they touched, all sinew and heat. Type specimen
and endling. Precious, I'm saying, then extinct. The fault
is not the shoulder's, warm or cold. The back is not the culprit,
even turned. Body is setting, not plot, whether burning or
burned. It's the farm I already bought, and now—field sown
with salt and somehow blooming—I'll have to live in it.

How the Night Ends

> You said I could have anything I wanted, but I
> just couldn't say it out loud.
>
> —Richard Siken

I didn't say sunrise, with its chatter song
and watery light, that stretch in the bedsheets.
I took the slighter sight, gave up sleep to see
the last bewildering second of night, when dawn

inhales but holds its breath. Nothing breaking
yet. Let's say it isn't the sun that snuffs out
starlight. Let's say twinkling ceases first,
flips its own switch with its own hand.

Imagine that volition. Understand—
in this version, night never touches day, never
boards the vessel that churns toward that other
landing, distant fire. *Like night and day*, we say,

when what we mean is *changed*, when what we are
is rocked back by the force of a thing become
another thing entire. I get it. But what about night
not as origin story for some other hero, not

the hunger that reaches for honey, but wanting
itself, unconsummate. Let's say you drop a stone
into the lake and the waves it makes don't
loosen, never lap the shore. Never mind aubade.

Forget aftermath and antecedent. I didn't ask
for more, for morning. Or night never ending or
the stopped clock. But I took every bit there was
of dark. Night ends, I learned, lightless as it starts.

IV.

I Can't Stop Thinking About that Sleepover at the Science Museum in 1987

First thing we unfurled our sleeping bags,
whole troop in darkened alcove among
fetuses afloat at every stage: pill bug,
pruned ear, prehistoric fish. I remember

how they seemed to me one baby,
that he might be out there now, somewhere
in the city, trying solid food or running
for mayor. That night, we stretched

like wires on our theater seats to see a man
in a high booth make lightning with the flick
of a switch, send a godbolt cracking between
two massive metal globes, Kelly's face aglow

and then aglow again beside me. In the morning
we stood at the incubator for a cosmic hour,
fogging the glass between our mouths
and the excruciating effort of those chicks,

slips of wet feather, to make the tiniest
holes in their dun-colored shells, and nobody
to help them—how can it be so hard
we thought, at least I did, just to get

born. But in that pocket universe, desperate
and divine, I touched the hand I wanted
for the first time. And in another room,
a ticker displayed the current population

of the earth. I was thirteen, stuffed full of
miracles I might not have been invited
to behold, almost kicked out of Girl Scouts
that week for unpaid dues, the binary

of life and death unfolding in real time:
somebody just got here, oh, look,
somebody's gone. It was a comfort then
to spend a span of afternoon in one last

dim-lit hallway, watching with Kelly
on a loop of film that fundamental
muscle pound and pound, a violence
I felt grateful for, so hungry

was this heart I knew it couldn't
stop, and the thing displayed so large
and low we might regard, without even
tipping our toes, its slick ventricles

chugging blood, the heat of which I felt
inside my body, too. This morning,
just divorced, I'd like to know again
what she did then, and not know

what she didn't, the kid I was before
what came to pass. Small and poor and queer
and here—with the whole world laid out
in pulsing dark before her. For her.

In Which I Reach for a Metaphor for Idealization and Find the Moon as Usual

It was *like* this: I was born wandering
a thick wood and came of age still
lost, so I called *beacon* the first light
I saw, followed it the way I'd tracked
the real thing on long rides home
from the lake as a little girl, mosquito-
bitten and sleepy on the back seat,
sticking to vinyl in my damp one-piece.
Beleaguered, I'm saying, as anyone
in skin, but I was beautiful, so I saw
beauty, even then. Through the window,
power lines seemed to move like
a jump rope swung between hands,
but it was me in motion, landscape
animated by the speed of my body
carried away. Haven't I always
been a poet? How practiced I am
by now in projection, throwing
my voice, my shine. For so long I made
odes to the moon I'd misrecognized,
catalogue of love songs for
the gorgeous pock-faced man slung
low in the night sky, his borrowed
swagger, irresistible secondhand
glow. I'd not yet felt the ocean roll her
tidal hips. I didn't know what a satellite
could do. Orbit? True. Turns out
even a body indifferent to yours can
do that. And what about the sun?
Never once looked in the mirror.

After

This morning, a hornet rode my wrist
for blocks. I felt uneasy but anointed.
I did not shake him off. Every summer
when I swam in the town pool
with my cousin, we tried to drown,
braid our eight skinny limbs so tightly
in the deep end we could not get loose.
I thought if I left my marriage,
I'd evaporate, so I kept quiet, sank
inside myself like a pocket stone. I still
don't know who's in the room with me
when I'm alone. I spent so much time
explaining that the dog, our child
were creatures with their own
wills, like him, that every living thing
wants to choose. Once, he pretended
to leave and I clung, said this doesn't
seem real, we love each other, you won't
be here when my liver burns out.
But in my head another voice said
don't talk him out of it. A door cracked
open through which I could see
nothing yet. As a kid, I didn't cry out
when I woke up scared. I worried
the stranger who came when I called
would look just like my mother. I mistook
everything I ever loved for something
else, but oh, the boozy draw of handing
over to a lover a body that's been a burden

since birth—hungry, touch-mad, unruly,
inconstant. Prey. He keeps asking who
I left him for. He doesn't know it's me.

Untouch

I watched the hands that worked the dough,
but I didn't taste the bread, breathed
sweetness while the others fed and shut
my mouth on *please.* Understood the flower
perfumed but failed to tip its blossom
to my nose. I saw wings through windows,
single-minded motion as they lit among
the branches of the shivered trees, but never
felt a body stir the breeze. Spun the fibers
into cloth but never donned the dress
nor took it off. Morning come, I sensed
the sun elucidate my room and didn't rise.
To close the space, untouch to touch—I tried.
Turned the knob a little—stayed inside.

Same, Girl

I have long felt dirty in God's sight—
not just naked but erased of skin,
my body a bag of lumps, jumble
of errors I can't hide. Seems
I am, to Our Father, a creature
sheer with grease and greed inside,
so I meant to shine under mortal
love's polishing eye. Fully satisfied.
Finally come clean, that scene.
Didn't happen. But this morning
in the wet grass I saw rotting
windfall pears clustered with bees
who, vibrating, seemed both
ravenous and surprised by their luck.

Still Life with Anhedonia

Listen, sometimes I do it because I don't know what
else to do, like when I'm overtired or I'm angry or sad
or I can't stop thinking or I just can't stop. If you know
me, it's possible I've done it in a room you were in,
I mean while you were there, and you didn't realize—
or Christ, if you did, thanks for not saying anything,
though let's be honest I might have been better off
if you'd said kid, Jesus, people can tell what's happening
under that blanket, give it a goddamn rest. I did a test once,
to see how many times in a row I could coax that bright
buzz, little obliteration. I don't remember the number,
half a dozen or so, but I recall a kind of numb
burning and also disappointment, not because I couldn't
keep going but because why would I. Honestly, why.

Whose Woods I Am I Think I Know

A creek runs crooked through me, clear and cold,
and there's myself submerged, although to swim
in one's own waters may to some seem strange.
I'm full of fruit, wild apples, serviceberry, a hive
of private bees that churns my nectar into gold,
for me. I'm told it's trespass. I hold no deed
besides my wet soil signed in tracks: rabbit,
black bear, fox. I've heard talk that down south
there's a tree that owns itself—by plaque decreed—
and still somebody put a fence around its trunk.
College kids get drunk and climb the links and carve
initials into bark. Meanwhile I stay quiet in this
outlaw dark, lovely to myself, and deep. What I don't
too loudly claim is mine perhaps I'll get to keep.

You Ask Me Why I Still Haven't Ordered a New Vibrator

and I tell you about the first cake mixes they tried to sell
in the 1940s—just add water and stir. The batter came out
creamy, cake as moist as mom's and maybe better,
but nobody bought. Why not? Too easy. What's dessert
mean if nobody spent her ingenuity and her afternoon
to make it taste just right? What if half of pleasure's
the greased elbow of the thing—or love? Particular hand
that makes a particular mouth sing? Eventually some genius
changed the directions so the mix called for one fresh egg,
and boom, enough work for the sugar to feel earned,
and muscle memory proves the technique's learned.
Makes sense to me. There's not always time for scratch,
a little arthritis in my wrist, but I don't want *too* instant,
either. I want the sweetest spot and just the right assist.

Vibrator Palinode

Yeah, I want the sweetest spot and just the right assist,
but drop the cake shit—that's not it. It's this: soon as
I've picked, possibility constricts. They make a rosebud
that sucks your clit. They make a dildo bent like a finger
that beckons from its box, and the Rabbit's so rumbly
reviewers say you'll never not get clocked. Anybody else
in the house? It's like a telltale cock. They sell a vibe
you can wear to work, work with your phone—
It's Bluetooth! There's an app for this bone! One's got
flexible wings that tuck beneath the lips, holding you
apart "like a tension rod in a doorway." The Arc, the Com,
the Dip, the Pom. Come on! It's an embarrassment
of dicks, to each of which I'd like to say, *Come in.*
                                        Choosing seems to me the only sin.

I Love So Many Things I Have Never Touched

but I'm not one of them. I like to cup
the silk and slighter heft of the breast
three years of suckling and decades
of gravity have emptied and stretched,
stroke the belly that droops uneven
below my navel, skin a little ruffled
there, soft as a pair of snagged hose
in the hand. When my fingertip finds
the coin of scalp surgery made bald,
I rub it like a polished stone and feel
safe. I love myself as I mean to love
the real and ravaged world from this
day forward—easy, yes, but fast.
I've been given a body. It won't last.

Sometimes I Say My Own Name—

sovereign, cityless, become citizen of sudden
wilderness, though it may sound like a song
I've heard you sing, first honeyed syllable,
little press on the *yes* of the second, so the *aah*
at the close conjures what you find when your
body finds mine. I start by saying my name
the way you do, like a question, not a key
but the soft tip of a single finger held to its lock,
and then I remember I'm in already, don't have to
slip past a sentry, don't even need to be sweet.
I was born with pleasure, that watchword, inked
on the soles of my feet. Sometimes—tonight—
I call for myself in the dark of myself, fearsome
and fulsome, and I come to myself like a light.

NOTES

The book's opening epigraph comes from *If Not, Winter: Fragments of Sappho,* translated by Anne Carson.

"Why I Am a Poet" borrows its title from William Stafford's poem of the same name.

"I Want to Go to Them and Say Stop" takes inspiration from Sharon Olds's "I Go Back to May 1937."

In "Home Training," I borrow the notion of "fatherless rooms" from Kay Ryan's *Synthesizing Gravity: Selected Prose.*

The title of "Who Is Responsible for the Suffering of Your Sister?" comes from Bhanu Kapil's *The Vertical Interrogation of Strangers.*

The epigraph for "Dear Life" comes from Linda Gregg's "Whole and Without Blessing."

The epigraph for "The Thing Itself" is a partially elided line from the "Notes and Queries" section of *The Guardian*'s website. In the body of the poem, I make brief, close paraphrase of passages from Leslie Fienberg's *Stone Butch Blues*, John Milton's *Paradise Lost,* and Helene Cixous's "The Laugh of the Medusa."

In "The Speaker's Husband," I reference Emily Dickinson's "Wild Nights—Wild Nights!," John Keats's "Ode on a Grecian Urn," and Anne Sexton's "The Double Image."

The epigraph for “How the Night Ends” borrows lines from Richard Siken’s “Litany in Which Certain Things Are Crossed Out.”

ACKNOWLEDGMENTS

I'm grateful to the following magazines for featuring poems from this collection, sometimes in slightly different forms:

Copper Nickel: "I Never Touch the Stuff but Oh It Touches Me"; *Gulf Coast:* "Dear Life" and "Why I Am a Poet"; *Image*: "The Thing Itself"; *Nashville Review*: "So What If I Was Born Wanting Both"; *Nelle*: "Home Training"; *Passages North*: "In the Other Universe, I Have a Bear Tattoo"; *Poet Lore*: "Sometimes I Say My Own Name—"; *The Rumpus*: "I'm Tired of Writing About My Childhood," I Want to Go to Them and Say Stop," and "What I Wanted to Keep Private"; *Salt Hill*: "I've Never Stopped Loving Anyone"; *Southern Humanities Review*: "Untouch"; *Southern Indiana Review*: "Interpenetration and Extension"; *Strange Hymnal*: "Second Person"; *Swamp Pink*: "When It's Over" and "It's Not the Body's Fault"; *32 Poems*: "Always I Have Been Trying to Show Her" and "How the Night Ends."

I'm grateful, too, to comrades who, with sharp eyes and gentle handling, made this book better than I could have made it alone: Anna Lena Phillips Bell, Malena Mörling, Maggie Hare, Hannah Bridges, Sarah Domet, and Lucas Cardona. And to August, for making it feel worth the work to make *everything* better.